Studies Of Trees In Pencil And In Water Colors

VERE FOSTER'S DRAWING-BOOKS.

STUDIES OF TREES

IN PENCIL AND IN WATER COLORS.

By J. NEEDHAM.

FIRST SERIES.

SEVENTEEN

EXAMPLES

IN PENCIL.

NINE

EXAMPLES

IN COLORS.

WITH A DESCRIPTION OF EACH TREE, AND
FULL INSTRUCTIONS FOR DRAWING AND PAINTING BY AN EXPERIENCED TEACHER.

CONTENTS OF FIRST SERIES.

STUDIES OF TREES

IN PENCIL AND IN WATER COLORS.

VERY Student who aspires to become a true artist, and even the amateur in art, should early cultivate a love for our Forest Trees, and seek to acquire an intimate knowledge of their forms, foliage, &c. The object of the present Studies is to describe the characteristic features of the various trees which form so charming a part of landscape scenery, and to enable the pupil to paint them with freedom and correctness. In the portions of the series already issued (*Easy Studies in Neutral Tints* and *Sketches in Water Colors*) the pupil was not hindered in his progress by an attempt to individualize the character of the trees depicted. But now, when it is hoped that satisfactory copies have been made of those more elementary examples, the pupil may be considered ready to learn how to paint each tree as it stands in the field or the forest.

In drawing a tree from nature it is of course impossible to represent in detail every leaf or twig; but the general mass, where it relieves against the sky or distance—the larger masses of light and shadow—the stem, the branches or arms as they leave the stem or are seen through the foliage, and the roots that grasp the ground—all these can be drawn. When we come to the detail of the foliage, however, it must be expressed in a species of shorthand, so to speak, that has been found by experience to be best suited to convey to paper the general effect of the tree itself.

Nevertheless it is desirable to study closely the shapes of the leaves, not only on account of their beauty and elegance, but to gain a knowledge of their varieties of form. This knowledge is of value to the artist, for there seems to be some analogy between the form of the leaf and the general aspect of the whole tree. For example, the rugged outline of the Oak leaf and the feathery spray of the Ash suggest the diverse characters and appearance of the trees themselves.

There are also other characteristics as important as the foliage. Much of the individuality of a tree lies in the trunk, especially in its ramification or mode of branching, and trees differ from one another in this respect. Another important feature, requiring the closest attention of the pupil, is the distinctive mode in which the masses of foliage are arranged on the respective trees.

In short, every tree has its own form, profile, expression, and character, almost as much as man and the lower animals, and we are now wisely taught to seek truthfulness and naturalness by individualizing the trees meant to be represented. In this Series of Lessons we do not include every species of British tree; we shall attempt to teach the drawing and painting of those only which are the more picturesque and common in landscape art, and which afford bold contrasts to one another in form, color, and expression.

A

GENERAL INSTRUCTIONS.

I N representing trees, either in pencil or color, the trunk and branches should be sketched first, and then the large masses of foliage. The next thing after the general outline, is to give the effect of *roundness* to the drawing. With this view observe carefully in what direction the light falls in the drawing about to be copied, and keep that in mind all through the work. The lightest boughs will generally be towards the centre, and the greatest dark also towards the centre, close against the lightest masses. In drawing a trunk remember that it should have, on its shaded side, the greatest depth given to it down the middle of the shade. This is required to give it the proper appearance of roundness.

The character of the bark is very important, and in the various trees there is much difference in this respect. Of this difference we will speak in each lesson, but the general remark may here be made, that the texture and distinctive markings must be more clearly shown where the light meets the shade. Most of our forest trees have their lower branches drooping towards the ground, the middle ones are thrown out horizontally, the upper branches trend more upwards in the direction of the main trunk.

In beginning to draw a tree with the pencil, great care should be paid to the light boughs, and their forms should be carefully sketched in. Then commence with the shade, working round the light shapes, those of the centre first, giving the greatest depth here, and towards the sides the shading becoming paler and the strokes more open; then work in the character of the light boughs close to the edge of the shade, making the character on the shaded side of these boughs a little darker than the shading; this will bring away the light boughs from the shade, making them stand out, it being the nature of the shade to retire, and the light to come forward.

There are two places where the distinctive character of the tree is most marked—all round the outer edges of its form, and also round the edges of all the light boughs. Towards the outer edge of the tree the foliage requires to be rendered with delicate sharp touches, and the shading should become more separated where the sky is seen through the tree.

The lead pencils used for drawing foliage must be of a good quality, so that markings made by them will bear rubbing out without furring the paper. H.B., B., and B.B. pencils should be quite sufficient for producing any of the effects required. The pencils should be carefully pointed; cut "chisel fashion," so that one edge will produce a fine line, and the other a broad one. The fine point can be obtained readily by steadily rubbing on a fine file or coarse sand-paper, as shown in the accom- 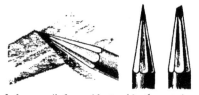 panying diagram. By changing the direction of the pencil from side to side the varying breadth of line shown in the figures can be easily produced. The pencil must be held at the proper angle to do this. A little practice will enable this to be done with ease; and *once the touch has been acquired*, the quicker the work is done the better.

INSTRUCTIONS IN DRAWING FOLIAGE.

WE have selected the Oak, Ash, Elm, Beech, Chestnut, Fir, and Larch as the trees for illustrating our special lessons on representing foliage by the pencil and the brush. These trees afford the greatest possible contrasts of form, color, and effect. Drawing foliage in pencil should always be learned before the use of the brush is attempted.

THE OAK.—The foliage of the Oak is disposed in irregular angular masses, the leaves growing in star-shaped clusters, requiring a touch which at once expresses their form and rugged character. Before attempting to draw the sprays, the zigzag lines at the upper left-hand corner (page 5) should be carefully imitated. This will be done most easily with the chisel-pointed pencil already described. A soft pencil should be used for the purpose. It should be held in a slanting position, and handled quickly and boldly. The paper should have a surface sufficiently rough to express the granulation visible in the example. A good deal of practice will be needed to acquire dexterity in making the zigzag touch in all directions, doing it over and over again on a large sheet of paper until it is learned. Then the horizontal mass, with the shadow on its lower side, should be persistently imitated until it is fully mastered. The branch and sprays filling the lower half of page 5 should now be drawn. Our young artist now finds himself drawing a portion of the tree itself. He must therefore commence by making a faint outline sketch of the whole, and then shade boldly, using the chisel point for the shadows and the fine side of the pencil for the outline, next the light. In these sprays the light comes from the right-hand side, and care must be taken to preserve the relative position of light and shade. Where the branches are under the masses of leaves, they will require the full darkness of the pencil.

THE ASH.—The first attempt should be the fan-shaped exercise in the middle of the left side of the example on page 6; then the two upper masses of spray, which must be practised till the hand can draw the left side quite as easily as the zigzag on the right side. It will be observed that these zigzags are really all little curved lines indicating the general pendulous drip of the extremities of the feathery leaves and leaflets. The rather horizontal zigzag lines of shadow will now be copied, and (after practising a whole page of them) let the central piece of shaded spray on the right of the example be attempted; it will be seen to be a junction of the two early parts of the lesson. Then the large branch below. Sketch its outline and the lines of its shadow with great care. All of this study should be drawn with an H.B. pencil, to express the light hue of the green, and should be done with the pointed side only, using the broader side of the pencil for the dark touches. The fan-shaped outline and wavy zigzags below are to convey the hint to the pupil that he may not have sufficiently learned the "trick" of the touch yet, and had better have more practice of its elements.

THE ELM.—The drawing of the Elm foliage is a process very different from that required for the Oak. While the Oak is all ruggedness and angularity, the foliage of the Elm consists of a series of rounded masses in which oval shapes predominate. The touch for rendering it in black-lead pencil partakes of that character. On page 7 are given a series of specimens showing how this touch is to be acquired. Commencing with the fan-shaped exercises in the upper right corner, and practising them till they can be done with facility, the pupil's next step should be to learn to do the connected touches to the left of these. The connected zigzag lines shown in the centre of the page have to be practised to give facility of expressing the shadow. It will be observed that the chisel-pointed pencil is not so necessary for the foliage of the Elm, or at least that the point need not be used quite so broad, as for the foliage of the Oak. The lower examples on the same page show the finished work resulting from the connection of the other lessons.

THE BEECH.—The expression of the foliage here (page 8) is quite different from any-thing we have yet attempted. The sprays are expressed by short horizontal touches, joined together by zigzag lines, also of a horizontal character, tending downwards in a slightly oblique direction. The small twigs and branches have, of course, a similar tendency.

In learning to portray the foliage of the Beech, the first practice should be the oblique very slightly curved connected touches, which are used to express the upper outline, then the shorter crisper zigzags used to denote the under outline of the sprays. These should be practised in both directions, from left to right and from right to left, to familiarize the hand with the drawing of both sides of the tree. Then the horizontal closer and darker lines, used to express the shadow side of the spray, should be similarly practised.

All the above exercises should be gone over again and again till thoroughly learnt; then the little tender trailing twigs; afterwards the full rich piece of spray which occupies the greater part of page 8 should be imitated. It will be found to consist of a repetition of the four examples on the same page, all joined together to give the drawing of an entire bough.

THE CHESTNUT.—The touch required for expressing the foliage of the Chestnut in black-lead pencil is somewhat similar to that required for the Ash, but as the leaves are much larger and more formal in shape so are their masses expressed by much bolder and larger touches. The tufts of leaves will be found to alternate from side to side of the small branches, and this arrangement will be observable in the first bit of practice at the top of page 9. The chisel side of a B. pencil had better be used, and the sort of curved, wavy, zigzag touch imitated as closely as possible. Then the overhanging fan-shaped outlines must be practised. These had better be done with an H.B. pencil, and when they are thoroughly learned the two complete sprays on the lower part of the same page may be drawn.

THE FIR.—The touch for the foliage of the Scotch Fir consists mainly of zigzag mark-ings with the sharp edge of a chisel-pointed pencil, held so as to give repetitions of short strokes almost vertical, sometimes curving to the right and sometimes to the left. The preliminary lesson on p. 10 shows this peculiar foliage. The pencil should be moderately soft, a "B.;" most of the work is done with the point, or by gradually turning the pencil round, to a position midway between the point and chisel side. The touches at the top of page 10 had better be imitated first, and then the bough in the middle. The lessons to the right and left afford specimens of the curious vagaries seen in the branches, which often curve downwards, and take a cork-screw twist round the stem.

FOLIAGE OF THE OAK.—Drawn by J. NEEDHAM.

FOLIAGE OF THE ASH.—Drawn by J. NEEDHAM.

FOLIAGE OF THE ELM.—Drawn by J. NEEDHAM.

FOLIAGE OF THE BEECH.—Drawn by J. NEEDHAM.

FOLIAGE OF THE CHESTNUT.—Drawn by J. Needham.

FOLIAGE OF THE SCOTCH FIR.—Drawn by J. NEEDHAM.

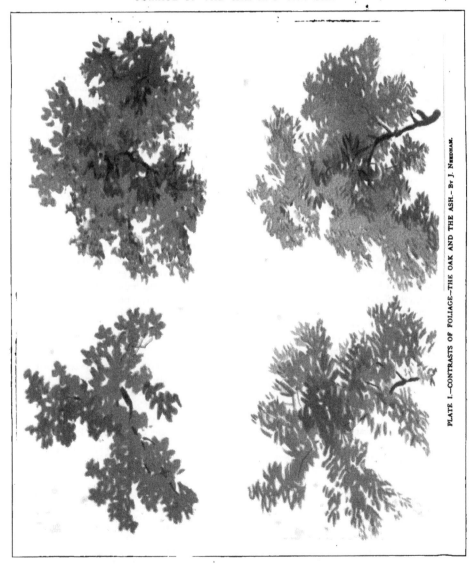

PLATE I.—CONTRASTS OF FOLIAGE—THE OAK AND THE ASH.— By J. Needham.

INSTRUCTIONS IN PAINTING FOLIAGE.[1]

IN order that comparison may be made between pencil and brush work required for the same trees, we now give specimens of the same foliage in color. We have placed the Oak and Ash together on Plate I., to show their great differences of effect and touch.

Great help will have been gained in the painting of the foliage by thorough practice of the examples in pencil. Although very different appliances are required for painting, yet the touch for the pencil being learned, that for the brush will not be found widely different.

We have already, in previous parts of this series, given the lessons in laying on washes and the manipulation of the brush, so we do not address pupils who are ignorant of the elements of painting in water colors. It is to be hoped that this practice has so familiarized our pupils with their work that this first lesson in painting will be found comparatively easy.

The green for the light boughs is composed of a mixture of Olive Green and Gamboge with a slight addition of Cobalt (or French Ultramarine). A small quantity of each color should be rubbed down on the palette, keeping each apart at first and blending them together as wanted, with a clean brush charged with clean water, and varying the tint by using a little more of the olive, of the yellow, or blue, according to the shade of green required.

PAINTING THE OAK.—Make a careful outline sketch of the first of the small colored examples on Plate I. It should then be painted with a middle-sized brush well charged with color, yet still retaining a perfect point and held almost upright. Great care must be taken to make clearly-defined touches and to leave the paper to be seen at many intervals through them. There are several tints of green in this exercise, and where they vary in coldness or warmth, the variation of tint required should be easily obtained by using more of yellow or of blue. The slight branches are given by Vandyke Brown.

In the second bit of practice the shadows should be laid in first. This tint is composed of a small quantity of Cobalt and Light Red, and the greens should be painted on top of it (when the grey is dry), but little holes should be left, as if accidentally, to allow the coldness of the grey to be seen here and there through the green touches. Care must be taken to give the effect of crispness and angularity to the foliage that is characteristic of the Oak. The branches and dark touches generally are to be done with Vandyke Brown.

[1] For brushes, black sables are best, as they possess greater elasticity than those made of camel's hair; but the latter sort of brush will also suit. The pupil should have four sizes of brush at hand, namely, "crow quill," "duck," "goose," and "swan." A large flat brush is also recommended. Other materials required have been noticed in the previous books on Water-color Drawing.

Moist colors are recommended; they suit as well as Cake colors for indoor painting, and are more convenient for out-door work. We enumerate the colors mentioned in the following pages :—

COBALT.	LIGHT RED.	INDIAN YELLOW.	VANDYKE BROWN.	CRIMSON LAKE.
INDIGO.	RAW SIENNA.	BROWN PINK.	OLIVE GREEN.	PINK MADDER.
FRENCH ULTRAMARINE.	BURNT SIENNA.	INDIAN RED.	SEPIA.	LAMP BLACK.
YELLOW OCHRE.	GAMBOGE.	RAW UMBER.	BROWN MADDER.	CHINESE WHITE.

The general advice given as to colors and mixture of tints, &c., is such as is approved of by Mr. Needham. But nearly every artist uses different combinations, and Mr. Needham wishes us to state that he would far rather that the young student should experiment for himself on the production of suitable tints, for in this way he will learn much, and even profit by his earlier mistakes.

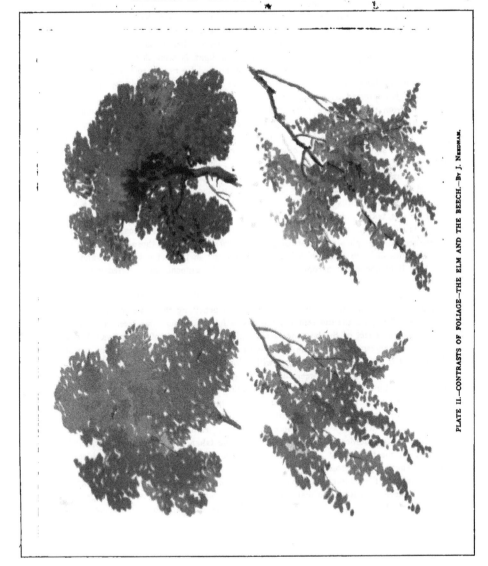

PLATE II.—CONTRASTS OF FOLIAGE—THE ELM AND THE BEECH.—By J. Needham.

PAINTING THE ASH.—On Plate I. are given two examples for painting the sprays of the Ash. These show how much their arrangement, form, and effect depend on a knowledge of the art of drawing their details properly, and the importance of having carefully attended to the lessons in pencil for the same tree. The delicate green used is much diluted, as the hue of the sprays of Ash partake more of yellow than of actual green. They are broken up in many varieties of angle and much light is seen through them, while the slight feathery nature of the leaves has to be expressed by the sharp touches (of the finely pointed brush) kept well separated. In the more shaded example, the tufty arrangement of the foliage is expressed by the second and third applications of the shadow, and this branch being lit from the left forms a contrast in practice to the pencilled branches on page 6. The touches of the brush are more elongated and more separated than those used for the Oak.

PAINTING THE ELM.—This tree in general effect and color is more sombre than the Oak, and not so varied in its tints of green. Olive Green deepened with a little Indigo will be required to express this general dark-green shade. The first exercise (Plate II.) is intended to teach the use of the brush for the whole tree, as well as to show how the sprays are to be treated where they show against the sky. The brush should be held almost upright and very full of color, and then worked with a number of independent touches producing a series of curved forms, taking great care to leave out the little interstices of light. In this example the branches are only faintly indicated, as they are actually eclipsed by the denseness of the foliage. In the second example several tints of green are worked in besides those used in the first one.

Touches of deep olive are subsequently applied; in the deepest shadow, and towards the high light, the green becomes almost black. The branches are painted with Vandyke Brown.

PAINTING THE BEECH.—This foliage requires a different touch from the preceding examples, but the practice we have already had in pencilling the same tree should simplify the work. Compare the different illustrations of foliage of the same tree. It will be seen how much the effect of the brush-work resembles the pencilling of the sprays. We cannot exactly draw zigzag lines with the brush as we can with the lead pencil, but we can use the finely pointed brush, when well charged with color, to produce a somewhat similar effect.

Rub down some Olive Green and Gamboge near one another, but separate, so as to vary the mixture if needed. A very little Indigo also, mixed with some Brown Pink, will give all the deeper tint that is necessary for the sprays. Let the touch be practised with a well-pointed brush fully charged with color and held almost upright. The color will thus flow freely, and when dry will be more transparent. A little more of the darker color will give the hue of the deeper touches. Care must be taken that this second working be not applied till the first is dry. A third hue of green will also be discerned, for which a little Burnt Sienna may be necessary.

When the first colored example has been copied the second may be attempted; it is merely a development of the first with some extra working of darker neutral green. The Indigo must be sparingly used, however; if overdone, it is apt to give a spottiness to the drawing.

PLATE III.—CONTRASTS OF FOLIAGE—THE FIR AND THE LARCH.—By J. NEEDHAM.

PAINTING THE FIR.—The foliage of the Pine family is as different from other trees in execution with the brush as it is in pencilling. We have placed our examples of the Fir and Larch trees on the same Plate, to show their contrast in form and treatment, although they agree in color.

Let a correct pencil outline be first made of both the colored examples. The outline sketch filling the lower left corner of page 10 is given to show the manner of outlining the paintings of foliage. In this case shading up with a pencil is inadmissible, but still a correct delineation must be made of all the salient form before coloring can be attempted.

In painting the foliage of the Fir, if the colors be applied in slightly different tints over one another while somewhat wet, the peculiar mottled appearance of the first example is obtained; the yellower shade floating into the bluer one,—these varied blendings giving the natural effect of the green of the tree. Great care is necessary, however, to preserve as many little bits of light as possible, and these spaces should be of the same shape as the touches of color. The brush should be a large one, well charged with pretty thick color, and flattened out by pressing it (on the palette and on the paper) firmly with the finger till it attains a serrated edge. The working of the brush must be applied so as to indicate the direction of the spiny leaves by a rapid turn upward. If the result should seem too mechanical and regular, a finely pointed brush can be used to mend and improve the work. The branches are to be painted with Burnt Sienna and a little Vandyke Brown.

In the second example the adding of the darker markings takes away any defects, and these darker touches have more of the Indigo in the composition of their green.

The painting of the Fir has much character and boldness in its treatment, and will not be found difficult to those who have bestowed care and diligence in following our instructions for drawing it in pencil. The green, being of a rather sombre character, is composed of Cobalt, Yellow Ochre, and a very little Burnt Sienna for the light boughs, and for the shade, Indigo and Olive Green. By varying the proportions of these all the different tints can be produced.

PAINTING THE LARCH.—The painting of the Larch is more a matter of adhering carefully to the exact form of a careful outline sketch, than of any craft in using the brush. It is mainly expressed, as shown in the first colored example on Plate III., by small crisp touches of a well-filled, sharply-pointed brush; greater care than ever being taken to preserve the lights and to impart the downward character to every touch, observing carefully the tendency of the boughs to curl up towards the end of the branches.

The second colored illustration shows how much of the necessary effect is given by the second and third workings of neutral color. The middle tint of cold green has been painted into the yellower one when it was still slightly moist; the deepest parts of shadow are represented by touches of very sombre color produced by the addition to the green color of a very little black. The greens for both these illustrations are composed of Olive Green and Cobalt in varying combinations, and with a very little Yellow Ochre.

NOTE. –A large sheet of Drawing Paper should be ruled in panels or squares, and covered with imitations of all the contrasting brush touches in the examples till perfection of copy is reached.

THE OAK.

A song for the Oak, the brave old Oak, who hath ruled in the green wood long!
Here's health and renown, to his broad green crown, and his fifty arms so strong!
There is fear in his frown, when the sun goes down, and the fire in the West fades out;
And he showeth his might, on a wild midnight, when the storms through his branches shout.
   Then sing to the Oak, the brave old Oak, who stands in his pride alone—
   And still flourish he, a hale green Tree, when a hundred years are gone!—*Henry F. Chorley.*

IN other lands the palm, the cedar, the gigantic Californian pine, are regarded as kingly trees, but in Great Britain the oak has by universal consent been adopted as an emblem of strength, majesty, and durability, and named the Monarch of our Forests. Nor need we wonder that the tree has attained this proud distinction. In our parks and forests, in broad meadows or narrow country lanes, in picturesque villages and woodlands, the Oak, with its stately trunk and massive branches and far-spreading foliage, almost universally forms a commanding feature of the landscape.

Not only in Europe but over a large part of Asia the Oak has held an important place in early religious and civil ceremonies. If not itself an object of actual worship to our ancestors, it was certainly an object of the highest veneration to them. Under its wide-spreading branches the Druid priests dispensed justice and performed their mysterious rites, and the Saxons held their national meetings. In former times, also, the acorn or fruit of the Oak formed an important part of the food of animals and even of men.

The tree belongs to an extensive genus of plants, many species of which have been introduced into Great Britain. The Common British Oak (*Quercus Robur* of botanists) attains a height of from 50 to 100 or 150 feet, with a thickness of trunk of from 4 to 8 feet. These are the ordinary dimensions; but many noble specimens of the Oak-tree, some of them historically celebrated, are found throughout Britain. In fact there is scarcely a forest remaining in England which has not some venerable trunk with a history or a legend attached to it. The great Winfarthing Oak in Norfolk, for the most part a ruin, but still producing foliage and acorns, is said to have been called the "old Oak" in the time of William the Conqueror. In 1820 its circumference at the extremity of the roots was 70 feet, in the middle 40 feet, and its age is believed to be fifteen hundred years. The King Oak at Windsor measured 26 feet in circumference at 3 feet from the ground, and is said to have been a favourite tree of William the Conqueror. The Shelton Oak near Shrewsbury was 26 feet in girth at breast height, and is celebrated as the tree from which Owen Glendower viewed the battle of Shrewsbury, fought in June 1403. At Boscobel House in Shropshire once stood a noble tree known as the Royal Oak, whose wide-spreading branches gave shelter to Charles II. after his defeat at Worcester in 1651. This historical tree has long ago disappeared, its huge bulk of timber having been carried off in handfuls by zealous Royalists.

B

Of slow growth, the wood of the Oak when matured becomes exceedingly valuable for its hardness, toughness, and strength, and it serves a greater number of useful purposes than almost any other kind of forest tree. For more than a thousand years British ships were mainly built of common oak until superseded by iron and steel. For durability the wood is almost unsurpassed, and it forms the chief timber used in all our buildings of high antiquity. What is called King Arthur's Round Table, in the county-hall at Winchester, is of oak, probably more than twelve hundred years old; it is 18 feet in diameter, and must have been cut from a tree of immense girth. The oaken doors of some of the chapels in Westminster Abbey are said to belong to the original Saxon church, and if so they must be over twelve hundred years old. The Shrine of Edward the Confessor in Westminster Abbey is of oak, and must be eight hundred years old. The roof of Westminster Hall, built in the time of Richard II., is of oak which is said to have been brought from Ireland. In the Irish peat-bogs many canoes, veritable "hearts of oak," have been discovered; some of them 40 feet long, and their antiquity would seem to carry us back to a period before the Christian era. The oaken piles of bridges built by the Romans in Julius Cæsar's time, across the Rhine and other rivers, have been found in recent times in perfect preservation.

When Shakespeare speaks of the "unwedgeable and gnarled oak" he well expresses the nature of the tree and the quality of its timber. These characteristics are derived from its slow growth and the twisting of its branches. In the latter feature it presents a great contrast to the ash, elm, poplar, beech, or almost any other tree. The Oak is further remarkable for the stoutness of its branches, which seem rather to divide from the trunk than to spring from it, as in most other trees. These, notwithstanding their natural tendency to twist, still continue their horizontal direction, and consequently when it has room to expand the tree will cover a wide expanse of ground. Its spreading roots also occupy a large area, and these often form a marked feature at the base of an aged tree, when the soil has been trodden away by men and animals to whom for ages it has afforded shelter.

The Oak varies much in appearance at different periods of its growth; perhaps in its aged state it interests us most; but our young artist must learn to draw the tree in every stage of development, and therefore we give a variety of illustrations of this most interesting tree.

On page 19 will be found a drawing of a tree in full development. This tree, hemmed in by its neighbours in the forest, has not had the opportunity of spreading as it naturally seeks to do, but it has compensated for this by growing taller than usual. The trees which formerly surrounded it have died or been thinned away, and now this fine tall Oak is seen to advantage. On page 21 is shown a comparatively young Oak, growing on a mountain side, where the soil is poor and rocky; and on page 25 a study of an old trunk in Sherwood Forest; on pages 51 and 52 are given bold sketches of Oaks from nature.

Our two colored illustrations (and the pencil-practice sketches) portray Oaks of widely different character: the one a scene in a dense forest, the other a widely spreading tree growing by the wayside, probably several centuries old, and illustrating the spirited lines which form a heading to this chapter.

FULL-GROWN OAK.—Drawn by J. Needham.

DRAWING THE OAK.—THE PENCILLED ILLUSTRATIONS.

WE have already given (page 3) a full description of the manner of drawing the foliage of the Oak. The study on page 21 (that of a comparatively young Oak growing on a mountain side where the soil is poor and rocky) forms a development of the lesson on page 5. The stem is now added from the ground upward. This drawing should be copied after the practice-page has been fully mastered. It contains all the various touches, but changed in direction or in relation of the light and the shadow, and will require good sketching in every point. The shading of the stem and branches must be carefully copied, and every bit of light left exactly as in the example. The distance must be kept pale, and the strong touches of shadow on stem and branches crisply touched in. The scrubby bank will need care, especially to preserve transparency by saving the lights between the touches. Should any of the little points of light be lost, they may be picked out with a very sharp penknife, or may be removed with a small pellet of clean bread rolled to a point between the finger and thumb.

On page 19 a finished pencil drawing is given of a tall, full-grown, graceful tree. The shading of the foliage is here expressed in a manner which gives greater richness to its effect —this is done by the flat intermediary tints which are produced by using the side of a flatly cut H.B. pencil under or before the bolder shading of a darker nature is applied. The darkest lines of the trunk and branches should not be executed to the last. By joining the instructions already given for foliage and trunk there should be no difficulty in copying this example, and it will materially aid in the sketching of the more difficult pictures described hereafter.

It is important, where any lights show themselves, to *save* them, as it were, by letting the paper be seen through. The bold touches of middle tints are produced by the H.B. pencil, and the heaviest of all are done by the decided use of the B. and B.B. pencils. The drawing of the slight sprays and the touches of the foreground should be well considered, and ought to be practised on separate paper till the necessary dexterity is acquired. Care must be taken not to let the darkest shadow on the trunk reach fully to the edges, but to preserve the rounded form of the trunk by a little light appearing towards the extreme outline. The drawing of an Oak-trunk on page 25 is a good lesson of the proper touch for the rugged bark possessed by the Oak. It must be boldly drawn, with a blunt-edged pencil, the point only being used for the darker touches of detail. The sprays can be easily added after the practice our pupil has had. The outline sketch should be carefully delineated, and the limits of the various projections and shadings very carefully but faintly drawn, before doing any shading.

The flat tints underlying the sharp dark touches are produced by the chisel side of an H.B. pencil, held sideways and rapidly moved backwards and forwards. The pencil must be held very lightly so as not to indent the paper, which thus, by the roughness of its surface, will give the appearance of the flat granulated tint of the originals.

MOUNTAIN SCENE—OAK.—Drawn by J. NEEDHAM.

PAINTING THE OAK.—THE COLORED ILLUSTRATIONS.

STUDY OF THE OAK-TRUNK.

BEFORE proceeding to paint the colored example, Scene in Sherwood Forest, we strongly advise the pupil (if he has not already done so) to make an accurate copy of the pencil study very similar to the principal object in this picture (see page 25). Further on in the work (page 52) will be found a still bolder pencilling of a very similar subject, and in this case the illustration is a facsimile of rapid sketching from nature. The bold sketch of the stem of an old Oak-tree should be used by the pupil as a first lesson for the drawing of the bark and gnarled trunk. It is intended to show how a sketch from nature should be done, and it is also a fine piece of practice for the colored pictures. The example on page 25 should, however, be the earlier practice, as the boldness and freedom shown in the sketch from nature can only be safely imitated by the hand which has already gained experience from diligent copying of the more finished study. If a pupil were to try to copy the bolder sketches first he would be likely to produce an unmeaning scribble, as it is only experience that can trust itself to do the bolder work after having gone through all the earlier lessons.

All these studies are by the same hand, and are treated in the bold, free style that is suited for sketching from nature. The practice gained by learning to depict the rugged bark, as in the pencil drawings, will facilitate the similar class of work when it comes to be done with the brush. A careful outline sketch should be made, and then the paler shading laid in by the use of the side of the pencil, as previously taught; then the middle depth, and, finally, the deepest touches. Recollect to keep the outer edge of the shadow side sufficiently pale to express the columnar shape of the trunk.

In the colored illustration, SCENE IN SHERWOOD FOREST (Plate IV.), we have a more interesting subject. A careful pencil sketch must be made—the distance so faintly drawn that the lines will be imperceptible by and by. The trunk and foliage near the eye may be more firmly pencilled, and here some of the stronger outline may be allowed to remain, so as to guide the final drawing of the rugged bark and masses of deeply colored foliage, when it comes to be represented with the brush. A wash of very faint Yellow Ochre should be applied over the whole paper when the sketch is finished. This will prevent the pencilling from smearing, and will tone down the harsh tint of the paper.

Once this is dry, the whole surface should be again slightly moistened, and the blue sky and clouds (Cobalt, Light Red, and a little Black) floated in at the proper places. Another faint wash (Cobalt tempered with a little Light Red) may be carried across the limbs of the tree where they have a cold tint, and in the same way used for the cool shadows of the distance.

The upper left corner of the picture is underlaid by a warmly tinted cloud; the grey should be very faint here, and may require a little more Ochre to warm it up. The blue sky and distance in the horizon should not be painted in at once in full force, but should

PLATE IV.—SCENE IN SHERWOOD FOREST.—By J. NEEDHAM.

be gained by repeated washings. All the cool shadows of the picture should now be laid in, working up to the light boughs, carefully giving them their forms, and marking well their characteristics at the edges, great care being taken to save out any lights that may appear.

The various shadows from the trunks are painted with Sepia, Indigo, Olive Green, and Light Red. The under tint of the foreground and middle distance is composed of Light Red and Yellow Ochre, faintly applied at first, and where the light falls on the ground tinted with a little Raw Sienna; Brown Madder and Olive Green being added where required.

Various cool greens, made of Yellow Ochre, Cobalt, and Black, will be required for the distance, in different combinations.

The warmly-tinted tree in the middle distance has an under tint of faint Raw Sienna, and the working on the top of it has a little Gamboge and Madder added to it. If the pupil have a difficulty in leaving out the lights at this part they can be taken out by a few touches of clean water at the last; the superfluous water is to be removed with a bit of clean blotting-paper, and the use, afterwards, of a piece of clean wash-leather rapidly rubbed over it when the paper has ceased to shine but is still slightly moist. The varying colors of the middle distance will require great care and accurate imitation. Yellow Ochre and Cobalt will give most of the requisite tints. The strong shadows may require a little development at the last, with some Lake and Cobalt for the purples and Sepia for the browns.

When all the distance is painted in, the foliage and branches of the main trunk may be proceeded with. A full knowledge of the painting of the Oak foliage, we hope, has been acquired from the practice-lessons and instructions on pages 11, 12. We need scarcely say that this earlier practice is absolutely necessary before the present picture is attempted. The vivid green, being mostly in shade, will be produced with Olive Green, Indigo, and a little Burnt Sienna; the strong shadows should be laid in first, and here the green should contain more of the blue in its composition. The detail being gradually heightened as the work goes on, the warmest and strongest markings are to be added last of all. Much of the bark has a ground-work of Yellow Ochre and Light Red, and Sepia with Brown Madder for the warmer parts, and a *very* little Indigo added for the cooler parts. Where the greenish hue appears a very slight wash of Olive Green can be passed over all, except where the little cool bits of light are seen. The lichens on the trunk will require some rich olive touches at the last. Where the net-work of branches appears against the sky both they and their leaves must be most carefully imitated. The little figure must be daintily added, when everything else is done, and the red cloak may be made rather more vivid Vermilion than the printer has given it.

STUDY OF THE FULL-GROWN TREE.

In order to call out the powers of our pupils at this stage, we advise them to make a copy of the same subject, but in pencil alone. It should be a good preliminary exercise to copy it in pencil drawing before proceeding to do it in colors. The touch is made up of all we have learned already, but this drawing should be done quickly, to show what experience has been acquired. Of course carefully make the sketch first, and then boldly

OAK—SCENE IN SHERWOOD FOREST. —Drawn by J. NEEDHAM.

go at the zigzag work, and seek to imitate it freely but by no means carelessly. At page 51 will be found a bold drawing of the same tree, but sketched from the opposite side, to give variety to the exercise. This also should be copied by the pupil before he attempts the colored illustration. The example on page 51 is intended to show the amount of work necessary in a rapid sketch from nature, but at the same time it will be found useful for preliminary practice in the sketching of the colored picture.

Having thus practised the light and shade, the colored picture of the OLD OAK BY THE WAYSIDE (Plate V.), now claims our attention. Commence by making an elaborate and careful sketch in faint outline. Note every touch of leaf and twig, and the position of the shade and cast shadows. The distant landscape must be delicately drawn, and the clouds outlined lightly and of course correctly.

Soften down all the sketching with clean bread crumbs, and then give a faint wash of Yellow Ochre over everything. The painting of the sky and distant scenery will, we hope, with the previous experience of our earlier landscape lessons, not offer any great difficulty. All the greys that underlie the sky and distance can be expressed with Cobalt and Light Red, with the addition of a little Lake or Pink Madder for the purples. For the heath, which has much sunlight passing over it, a little Yellow Ochre, Burnt Sienna, and Brown Madder is necessary; these three colors (or any two of them) will give all the sunlight that is required. The patches of grass, enriched with the heather bloom, can all be given with the same colors, heightened perhaps with a few touches of Vandyke Brown and Olive Green.

As the general tint of this picture is a warm one, the first wash over the whole paper may be a little richer than usual, and in this case the wash of Yellow Ochre may have a very little Light Red added to it. It is well to paint in the shaded side of the foliage first, working up to the light boughs, and in doing so to carefully give to the edges their proper form and characteristic crispness of outline. All shade should be deepest in the middle of the tree; towards the outer edges the shading must be more separated, because the sky is seen through the leaves and branches. We have to impress upon our pupils that, as the character of the tree is best seen round the edges of the light boughs, so great pains must be taken at the edges to adhere to the form and touch in laying in the shadows and detail of the leaves.

The foliage forms the most important part of this picture. An honest study and vigorous copying of the lessons on page 11 will make all this work simpler than it appears at first sight. We would, however, advise our young pupils to practise this part of the work on separate paper, each bough by itself, before they attempt the finished drawing.

The greens in shadow can all be produced by Olive Green, Indigo, and a little Burnt Sienna, in varying proportions. The lighter boughs, where tipped by the sunlight, will require warmly tinted greens, and these can all be produced by Olive Green, Gamboge, and Cobalt. However, a very little Burnt Sienna may have to be added, to supply the brownish tint, and give force, by contrast, to the masses of yellowish green.

The trunk has an under tint of very pale Light Red and Burnt Sienna. Over this

PLATE V.—OLD OAK BY THE WAYSIDE, SURREY.—By J. Needham.

some pale Olive Green and Indigo will be needed for the shadow side, while the markings of the bark and most of the branches of the tree are done with Vandyke Brown, deepened where required with a very little Indigo. The general detail of the foreground and middle distance will require careful treatment, and is mainly done with Vandyke Brown, with a little faint Cobalt Blue added for the distant detail—care must be taken not to overdo its strength so as to cause spottiness.

Here and there on the right side of the tree some decayed twigs show themselves out against the shadowed foliage; if the pupil fail to leave these out, as he very likely will, they can be "taken out" by the use of a very finely pointed brush charged with clean water, and the use of wash-leather, as previously described, or they can be drawn in neatly with a little Chinese White, which, when dry, can be glazed over with a little pale brown, yellow, or green, as the case requires. The same method may be adopted to give value to a few of the touches of brilliant yellow-green on the extreme edges of the light sprays in the centre of the tree, which may have been lost by the inexperienced hand of the young artist.

We hope we have said enough to enable our pupil to succeed in making fair copies of these beautiful forest scenes. If he can produce a better imitation of the pictures by means of any other colors, by all means let him do so, but first let him try how far he can succeed with those mentioned above. Mr. Needham's plan with his own pupils is to leave much of the mixing to themselves, once he has told them of the plan he adopted himself. This system calls out the talents of the pupils, and has frequently been productive of surprising results, successful and otherwise.

No young artist ever learned the trick (for it is little else) of expressing the foliage of the Oak by the brush without less or more failure at first, and many trials of patience may be necessary; but once it is learned, it is not readily forgotten. And—what may be encouraging to beginners—is the fact that, once the knack of painting the Oak spray has been acquired, that of nearly every other tree becomes a comparatively simple matter.

THE ASH.

THE Common Ash (*Fraxinus excelsior*) is a native of Great Britain, an important timber tree, and one of the finest objects in our rural scenery. Inferior, perhaps, to some trees in robustness or grandeur, yet for height, gracefulness of form, and elegance of foliage, it has few or no superiors. Speaking of the Ash as a landscape decoration, Mr. Grigor says " it is nearly perfect. The whole outline is easy, and in a good specimen we look in vain for anything lumpish or rigid." Indeed, authors both ancient and modern, agree in their admiration of the beauty of the Ash-tree. Virgil calls it the "fairest of the forest." Gilpin speaks of the beauty and lightness of its foliage, and the fine, easy, flowing line of its stem and branches. Sir J. Dick Lauder considers it a "noble and magnificent tree;" and Strutt, whilst admiring its beauty in tranquil scenery, says, "it is in mountain scenery that the Ash appears to peculiar advantage, waving its slender branches over some precipice which just affords its soil sufficient for its footing, or springing between crevices of rocks; a happy emblem of the hardy spirit which will not be subdued by fortune's scantiness."

The Ash grows rapidly, and reaches in fine examples a height of about 80 feet, with a trunk 4 to 5 feet in diameter, but many specimens of even larger growth are to be found. Loudon mentions several Ash-trees from 20 to 30 feet in circumference, with a height varying from 70 to 90 and even 100 feet. The great Woburn Ash is 90 feet high, 23½ feet in circumference at the ground, with a clean stem of 28 feet. In Wiltshire there are many trees with clean stems of 50 feet, and from 9 to 12 feet in girth. An Ash-tree growing at Carnock, in Stirlingshire, planted about the year 1596, is 90 feet high, with a circumference at ground of 31 feet.

In olden times some superstitious usages were associated with the Ash. Children suffering from certain diseases were passed through large fissures made in the tree, which were then filled up with loam, and if the parts in time closed properly, the little patient was held to be cured. Another practice was to bore a hole in the tree, in which was placed a living shrew-mouse, and the hole then filled up. Such a charmed tree was called a "shrew-ash," and a few strokes with one of its branches was accounted a sovereign remedy against cramp and lameness in cattle.

An idea remains—possibly a relic of these darker times—that an Ash exudes some liquid which is hurtful to the growth of anything underneath the tree. But this is quite a fallacy. Its roots are remarkable for their tendency to take a horizontal direction, and being abundantly furnished with fibres which approach closely to the surface of the ground, they thus absorb almost all moisture and effectually check the growth of other vegetation. The Ash is therefore not a tree to be allowed to grow round gardens. Its roots dislike the presence of stagnant water, but delight to approach as closely as possible to the gravelly bed of a running stream. Owing to these instincts, if they may be so called, the Ash outstrips any other tree when it grows on the shallow rich soil which borders the course of our mountain streams.

The wood of the Ash is especially valuable for its toughness and elasticity. Its qualities were well known to the Greeks and Romans, the latter of whom employed it in the making of weapons and implements of husbandry. In our own day the carpenter, the wheel and cart wright, the turner and cooper, and especially the agricultural implement maker, all find the wood excellent for their various purposes. When properly grown it fetches nearly as high a price as the best oak. In ancient times the keys or seeds of the Ash were held in high repute by physicans for their medicinal properties. Evelyn says they were also when green pickled and preserved as a " delicate salading."

Like most other trees the form and general appearance of the Ash are affected by the situation in which it grows. When grown with other trees it usually rises with a clean straight stem to a great height before the head begins to expand, the side branches decaying and being thrown off at an early period for want of room. When unencumbered by other trees, though it generally carries up a leading stem, it throws out numerous side branches; these at first grow at an acute angle with the trunk, but, as they increase and lengthen, the weight of foliage and additional spray causes them to bend and take a sweep, thus producing that depending spray and foliage so much admired in the full-grown Ash.

The leaves of the Ash differ in form from those of many trees: botanists term them *pinnate* or feather-shaped, and they are composed of about five pairs of long narrow leaflets with a terminal odd one. This form of leaf gives the tree, when in full foliage, a soft appearance as if it consisted of masses of plumage, and it is this characteristic of lightness and softness that contrasts so beautifully with the more massive foliage of other trees. But this softness and feathery appearance, while most acceptable to the artist for its beauty, renders the Ash a most difficult object to properly portray with the pencil.

The foliage of the Ash is very late in making its appearance, consequently in early spring the tree cannot compete in beauty with other forest trees which have been more active in donning their green attire. It is equally remarkable, too, for being among the first of our trees to shed its foliage. On this point Gilpin remarks that its leaf is much more tender than that of the oak, and sooner receives impressions from the winds and frost. In its early decay we sometimes see its leaf tinged with a fine yellow, which contrasts well with the neighbouring greens, and helps the effect for the artist. Sometimes, on the other hand, in a sheltered situation when the rains have been abundant, the Ash will retain its light pleasing green when the oak and the elm in its neighbourhood have caught their autumnal tints. Gilpin also remarks upon the exceeding elegance of the sprays, branches, and main stem of the Ash, that they hold their course, continuing a beautiful sweep throughout the whole tree, which frequently gives a gracefulness of form, in direct contrast to the angular ruggedness of other trees.

FULL-GROWN ASH.—Drawn by J. Needham.

DRAWING THE ASH.—The Pencilled Illustrations.

WHEN treating of the contrasting touches required for foliage, that for the Ash has been fully described and illustrated (pages 3, 6), but it will be well to repeat the essence of the earlier lessons for this tree, as it is one of the difficult trees to draw *properly*, and requires a slight airy touch that will only come by experience. Indeed, after having drawn the rugged foliage of the Oak, it will be well to revert to the examples of the Ash on page 6, and go over all the practice of the upper part of the page anew. The foliage is as different from the Oak as it is possible to be, and the touch as different in consequence. The pencil must not be held so stiff or so erect as for the Oak, and the point is more used than the chisel side of the pencil. When the touches on the upper part of page 6 have been fully acquired, the bough in the centre of the same page may be sketched and drawn with great care. In order to acquire the airiness and freedom of style which this graceful tree demands, it will doubtless need to be drawn several times. If our pupils will diligently practise the early examples, then the more extended example (BRANCHES AND SPRAYS, page 33) should offer no difficulty. This pretty drawing displays the branches and sprays of the upper part of the tree, and it should be a pleasure to copy it. The Ash exposes more of its limbs and the general contour of its branches than most other trees, and in the above example this peculiarity is well expressed. Most of the leaves are shown in shadow against the sky, and are therefore more easy to imitate. The stems and branches, in the drawing, have the light and shade on their surface beautifully distributed, and in copying this, care must be taken to convey, by the direction of the touches, the vertical veining of the bark. The upward and downward curves of the leading lines of the sprays must be carefully imitated, as the example exactly expresses the growth of the tree in this respect.

The drawing of the FULL-GROWN ASH on page 31 shows the tree well clothed with foliage, when the leaves are fully expanded. Much will depend on a very accurate outline sketch being made for this drawing. The position of every bough, branch, and tuft of foliage must be defined; if left to the hap-hazard chance of being done with the shading, without the guiding outline, the result will be a mass of confused lines, with all the unity of the drawing lost. The tufted masses of foliage are in this example seen to be more connected, and assume forms resembling rich plumes of ostrich feathers. The very light pale green of the masses of leafage are expressed in black and white by showing the paper as much as possible, while the pinnate character of their shape has to be carefully defined by properly drawing the outline of the general form and also carefully drawing the edges of the shadows. The shaded side of the tree must have myriads of bits of light left. One can always see little patches of sky through the outer foliage of an Ash more than in most other trees. The outer touches and the hanging sprays must be given with great character. The distant trees possess a soft but pale flat tint, through which, however, the stem, branches, and shadows must still be discernible; this part and the distant landscape must be kept as pale as possible,

BRANCHES AND SPRAYS OF THE ASH.—Drawn by J. NEEDHAM.

and great care should be taken not to overdraw the outline of the light spray, where the distant tree impinges upon it.

The example of the OLD WEATHER-BEATEN ASH on page 37 may portray one of those trees which were applied to superstitious uses in the times of our great-grandfathers, as described by Gilbert White. However, whether it has been rent by time or by violence, it is a very picturesque specimen of an ancient tree. It will be observed that what remains of the bark possesses the same kind of markings as were borne by the tree in its youth, in regard to which we have already given instruction. The lower arms and stem have lost nearly all their graceful outlines, but the foliage buds forth as fresh as ever. The upper branches still maintain the characteristic graceful curves of the younger tree. This tree has been pollarded in its middle age, which is a kind of severe treatment that can only be applied to the willow with success. To any other tree it is utterly fatal in the matter of beauty of form and other picturesque elements. The dark mass of shadow in the hollow trunk should be made the greatest depth in the drawing, so as to show out the greenish-grey tint of the bark of the old tree. Care must be taken to preserve the little points of light. The gnarled roots will require careful drawing.

PAINTING THE ASH.—THE COLORED ILLUSTRATIONS.

I T should hardly be necessary to impress upon our pupil that to succeed in copying even a simple drawing like that on the opposite page, a most careful pencil sketch will be essential, in which all the minutest details must be noted. A dull olive color is the prevailing tint of the stem and branches of the Ash generally, but this varies in different specimens; sometimes the hue of the surface may be a reddish brown or dull yellow tint or even a pale grey, according to the situation being dry, or moist, to facilitate the growth of various lichens.

The colored illustration of the ASH BY THE WAYSIDE (Plate VI.) is generally of rather a warm tint, and the trunk is also of a richer tone than usual. To impart this a very thin wash of Light Red will be first applied all over the sketch, the learner taking care to have it very faint or entirely omitted where the cold shadows and greenish tone are apparent. It is an evening effect, and a warm tone of sunset pervades the landscape. The sky, middle distance, and foreground are all treated in the light sketchy style which characterizes most of the studies of this Series. We would like our pupil to imitate this manner as much as possible. The sky, and indeed most of the picture, will require a little more than usual of the warm wash of faint Yellow Ochre tinged with Light Red and Cobalt, and a very little Black will give the deeper neutral tints of the clouds and middle distance; Pink Madder and Cobalt will supply the neutral purples; and a very little Pink Madder alone with some Yellow Ochre added to it will supply its warm and faint ruddy tints, and also those of the clouds. The yellow bank behind the figure will have an extra wash of Yellow Ochre mottled with a very little Raw Sienna; the same will be required for the bank on the right, warmed subsequently with a little Sepia and faint Brown Madder. Sufficient depth must be given to the neutral grey shadow across the road.

PLATE VI.—ASH BY THE WAYSIDE.—By J. NEEDHAM.

It is now time to attend to the tree itself, the branches at the upper part of which should receive, where requisite, their neutral grey. The general dull olive tint will be produced by a faint wash of Olive Green cooled with a little Sepia; some stronger olive will be required in various parts of the trunk where the mosses cling; and later, Vandyke Brown tinged with a little Olive Green for the stronger touches. Care must be taken to stop out the various little lines and markings, so as to allow the original faint washes of Olive Green, of Light Red, and of grey to be seen through. When the detail of the branches is complete, then the sparse foliage must be sharply painted in with a neutral green composed of Burnt Sienna and Indigo with a little Gamboge added. The distant tree behind the trunk should be painted with a brighter green, but kept faint to indicate the distance.

If in painting the large trunk the little bits of light where the warm yellow grass shows before the base of the tree have been lost, the spikes of grass can be painted in with a little Chinese White, glazed when dry, with a touch of Yellow Ochre or Naples Yellow; this corner, part of the foreground, the bank on the right, and the withered trees which spring from it, may require to be enriched by a faint wash and some subsequent touches of Brown Madder. The figure must be vigorously put in, and will be found to make the landscape retire behind it, while by contrast it causes the shadow on the road to seem much more faint. The figure also imparts life to the little picture, and causes the size of the large trunk to be more correctly estimated. This study, being mainly of the trunk and branches, does not so much need the foliage lessons already given on pages 11 and 14, but still the slight pointed touches there taught should, if they have been carefully practised, be easily applied to the leafage of this drawing. In our next example the use of these preliminary lessons in foliage will be more apparent.

The GREAT ASH shown in Plate VII. (page 39) contains rather more surrounding detail and also more manipulation of foliage, and may prove a little more difficult than some others of the Series; but this must not deter our pupils from doing their best to make a faithful copy of it. To attain success we would in the first place enjoin the necessity of a most minute outline sketch being made, not only of all the varying lines of color in the sprays and leaves in shadow, but also of the branches, trunk, and landscape. When this is thoroughly done the sky and distance can be gone on with. This drawing will bear the first warm wash over the whole paper being somewhat stronger than usual. The clouds, distance, and foreground can be painted in with their earlier washes while the paper is moist. Cobalt, Light Red, and Black will give all the greyish tints for the clouds, the shadows of houses, and the distance and underwash of the principal shades in the landscape and foreground. The same neutral grey can be carried over the shadow side of the foliage and the cool parts of the trunk.

A very faint wash of Light Red or Pink Madder will supply the warm tones of the middle distance, a little Cobalt and Light Red will give the detail of the distant foliage, and the same (used stronger) for the trees on each side of the distant road. When quite dry this foliage may be warmed with a little Yellow Ochre, and the road and distant hill in the faint sunlight will require the same treatment. The detail of the buildings will require to be very neatly done with a similar purplish grey to what has already been used for the detail

OLD ASH-TRUNK.—Drawn by J. NEEDHAM.

of the landscape, and the same for the detail of the foreground, a little Sepia being added
for the darker markings. Some Olive Green will be required to impart the prevailing tint
to the trunk of the Ash; this will be observed to show through the darker touches in the
original, and the amount of olive in the tint is shown in that limb of the tree which is
immediately over the porch of the house to the right. The foliage may now receive our
attention. The practice-lessons on page 11 should have simplified the touch required for the
brush-work; but if the pupil feel any difficulty, let him not attempt the painting of this part
of the present picture until he is proficient in the theory and practice of the earlier lesson.
When the boughs come to be painted, the cool neutral greens of the shadows had best be
painted first. This is a very large tree represented on a small scale, and all the touches
must partake of a much more minute character than anything we have yet attempted. It
must necessarily be done with a small brush, but the brush must be well charged with color.

The high-lit greens are made of Olive Green and Indigo with Gamboge in varying
proportions where required, and the shaded greens are Olive Green and Indigo. There will
require to be a number of workings of the various tints of greens, and in all of these, however
minute, the feathery character of the spray must be maintained. Care must be taken to
preserve the lights and to lessen the work in each color in proportion to its depth; that is
to say that the deeper the shade of green the less of it should be used. The brighter washes
are first applied, and the masses of the shadowed side of the tree may next be attended to,
beginning with the parts where the deepest shade is seen. Before these are filled up, as we have
said, a wash of bright green will have been applied over all the portions of the tree that are
supposed to be lit by the sunlight. This wash (Olive Green, Gamboge, and Indigo) should not
at first be deeper in tint than that of the high lights of the brightest spray in the centre branch.

The whole can subsequently be toned down by another deeper wash of the same colors
but with a slight russet hue (imparted by the addition of a very little Brown Pink), great care
being taken to leave at the extreme edges of each mass of light-colored foliage the least
possible line of the original light wash shining through the later one. In this way the detail
of the foliage must be carried on, a slightly deeper wash of green being added where necessary,
always retiring from the bright edges and gradually working in towards the shadow underneath,
till by this means a succession of varying tints is obtained. On the top of these washes a
number of minute darker touches will be required still, in all of which the feathery construction
must be recollected. All the necessary tints of green can be made with varying mixtures
of the pigments already named. It will be well to test the tint of each mixture on a separate
piece of paper before using it.

Should the eye be fatigued by the minute work of the foliage, it would be better to
leave it for a little, and devote attention to the detail of the trunk or of the middle distance
or foreground. Much of the detail of the trunk will be rendered by Sepia, Light Red, and
Olive Green, to impart the prevailing hue of the bark, but none used too strongly. The
branches immediately under the foliage, with the dark touches of blue-green, will require
to be carefully copied; indeed, much of the effect of the whole tree depends upon success in
this part of the work. By their strong contrast these branches express the overhanging

PLATE VII.—THE GREAT ASH.—SCENE IN SURREY.—By J. Needham.

character of the "broad green crown" which is the distinguishing feature of this fine old tree. The bits of sky seen peering through at this part should be carefully imitated, and no amount of care in subsequent "taking out" will give the same effect as leaving them out at first. We may remark that these strong touches of deeply shaded foliage have rather more Indigo in the composition of their green than we have yet used; still they must not be as dark as the deepest shadows of an elm would be, where we would have to use a little Black to render the shadows sufficiently sombre.

Some of the lightest bits of the spray in the original painting by Mr. Needham were given with slight decided touches of body color, and therefore we cannot expect the pupil to do entirely without its use, but it must be confined only to the parts of the central bough which are in strongest light. This should be done with Chinese White tinted with Naples Yellow, and tinged at the last with the least possible tint of the faintest Cobalt to convey the necessary amount of greenish hue. It should be done with a very fine brush, and only applied at the tips of the sprays. If overdone it will kill all the other greens and spoil the picture.

There is a little hanging spray falling upon the trunk which may require to be "taken out" and to have one or two touches of the opaque color, but not so brilliant as that described above. Some of the branches under the large bright spray are represented as catching the light. These are very necessary to the picture, and if they have not been "saved out," as they ought to have been, may now be taken out by the use of water, blotting-paper, and wash-leather.

The tree should now be complete. The tiling (and the brickwork where it shows) of the houses, the walls in the middle distance, the buttressed wall on the left, and the figure, may need a little Light Red and a very little Brown Madder to warm them up. The road needs a little Raw Umber to give it color. The smaller figures and the cart in the distance should be daintily put in, if they have not been already done.

The blue of the sky when the foliage is all painted may seem a little weak by contrast, and may need some more working. The figure under the tree must be done with care— the cloak may be a little brighter than it is in the example; this will tone down the reds in the landscape, which it is probable have been printed rather strongly. The gravel on the road in the foreground can be rendered by a little Vandyke Brown applied by dragging a nearly dry brush across the grain of the paper. The markings at the foot of the tree, the yellowish patches of scant grass, the bit of sward in front of the cottage, will need neat work and careful imitation. Where the little bits of cool light strike the roots from which the bark has been trodden away, the pale fleshy color of the exposed wood, lights up and gives sparkle to the foreground, and must be carefully copied.

THE BEECH.

OUDON states that the Beech (*Fagus sylvatica*) is a native of the temperate parts of Europe, and is also found in some parts of Asia. In Switzerland it occupies the south sides of the mountains which have their north sides clothed with the silver fir. The tree grows luxuriantly in England, chiefly in the chalk districts; but it is not indigenous either to Scotland or Ireland. It is the national tree of Denmark, where it flourishes vigorously.

In favourable situations the Beech generally attains the height of 70 or 80 feet, with a trunk 5 or 6 feet in diameter. Instances are recorded, however, of the tree attaining 100 feet, and when allowed ample growing space the diameter of its trunk and spread of its branches are at least equal to any other forest tree grown in this country.

As an ornamental tree the Beech has high claims. Its stem is massive and powerful, its bark smooth and of a silvery cast, and when the heat of summer unfolds its silken foliage it displays a verdure rich in softness and delicacy. "It is when seen in the full luxuriance of its summer foliage that the Beech is most admired; at this season it is, if a solitary tree, a mass of shining deep green from the ground to its summit; and the lover of nature who has taken refuge in a grove of Beeches from the sultry heat of a cloudless summer's day will not fail to experience that inexplicable feeling of sadness, mingled with longing, which the contemplation of nature's greater works always excites."

In England the Beech forms extensive forests of great beauty. In the vicinity of London there are many groves of these trees, but perhaps the best known are the celebrated Burnham Beeches, near Windsor, which have lately been purchased with their surroundings by the Corporation of London, and thus a most interesting and picturesque addition has been made to the parks available for the enjoyment of the citizens of the overcrowded metropolis. This fine Beechwood is believed to be all that remains of a vast forest that anciently extended into Surrey. Most of the trees have been pollarded, and many of them are mere hollow trunks, yet seeming to be in vigorous health. For although the vigour of the tree rarely extends beyond one hundred and fifty years, examples are plentiful of a much greater age. An old Beech in Windsor Park, still in life but a ruin, is said to have existed before the Norman Conquest; and the celebrated "Pontey's Beech" at Woburn Abbey in 1837 was 100 feet high, with a clear trunk of 50 feet. Fine specimens of the tree are to be found in Yorkshire, and even so far north as Morayshire.

The timber of the Beech is not generally valuable. It stands well under water, and is used for piles, flood-gates, and sluices; also in the manufacture of chairs, carpenter's planes and other tools, shovels for maltsters, and wooden rollers. It is also used for smoking fish and as railway sleepers. It makes good firewood, and its charcoal is esteemed for the manufacture of gunpowder. The wood will take a high polish. The nuts or fruit of the tree afford in autumn choice food for the deer, pheasant, partridge, &c.

D

The Beech was particularly admired by the ancients, who luxuriated in the lofty canopy afforded by its dense foliage. The Roman poets had evidently a high opinion of the tree. They describe it as being lofty, furnished with wide-spreading branches casting a dense shade, loving the hillside, attaining a great age, and furnished with a bark so smooth that rustics selected it to carve their names on, and even for the reception of their poetical effusions.

In modern times, however, its claims to the possession of picturesque beauty have been disputed by some authorities. Though it may be difficult for the painter to represent it in such a way as to produce a pleasing effect on the mind, the Beech is notwithstanding a noble tree in nature. "Whatever may be the defects of the Beech in composition," says Selby, "and defects we allow it to have, it possesses too many important advantages in itself to be set entirely aside or banished from our parks and lawns. Its noble and majestic size, its umbrageous and thickly clothed head, affording in summer heats a cool and welcome shade, and which, though without the tufted beauty of that of the oak, or the feathery lightness of the ash, is valuable for the depth it produces in distant scenery; the beauty of its foliage, either when matured and reflecting in gem-like coruscations from its deep green polished surface every play or scintillation of light, or as it first bursts from its envelopes, tender in hue and delicate in texture; the smoothness as well as the light and pleasant color of its bark, which catches and produces those sparkling lights we so oft admire in the stems of a beechen grove,—are all of them strong and powerful recommendations in its favour, and must always counterbalance its minor defects, and those deficiencies which detract from its merits as an artist's tree."

The Beech generally preserves its form and balance remarkably well, as it is not so liable as many other forest trees to suffer from storms of wind and snow; its limbs and larger branches, from the angle they form with the trunk, presenting less leverage, and the slender nature of its spray offering much less resistance than where it is heavy and thick.

Mr. Johns says there are several singular varieties of the British Beech in cultivation which deserve notice. The Purple Beech has its leaves in their early stage of a bright rose-color, which, as the season advances, deepens to a rich purple approaching black. It is a native of Germany, where it was discovered about the middle of last century. This variety presents a beautiful appearance when scantily interspersed among other trees in a lawn or grove, but should never be planted alone. The Cut-leaved Beech has its leaves indented, so as almost to resemble in shape the leaves of a fern. The Weeping Beech is said to be the most elegant tree of British growth. In a gentleman's park in county Tyrone are some specimens of this tree whose trunks measure upwards of 10 feet in circumference, and the branches, which extend 50 feet from the stem, touch the ground. There is also a fine specimen in the drive called the Hobby at Clovelly in North Devon.

PLATE VIII.—THE BEECH IN EARLY AUTUMN.—By J. Needham.

DRAWING THE BEECH.—THE PENCILLED ILLUSTRATIONS.

A T pages 4 and 8 we have given instructions how to draw the foliage of this characteristic tree. The early practice consists mainly of horizontal touches, and a similar treatment of the pencil will be found necessary for expressing the smooth surface of the trunk.

Mr. Needham has given us a charming selection of studies of the Beech, mostly taken from the celebrated Wood of Burnham, near Windsor. We will now treat of these in detail.

The large drawing on page 45 of a row of Beeches will require careful sketching and some thoughtful study before the shading is commenced; the distant foliage should be done with the chisel-side of an H.B. pencil, and the branches drawn in on top of the shading in a firm, decided manner. The key of the effect in this drawing lies in the second tree, which is in deep shadow, and by its bold contrast "brings out" the tree in the foreground, and at the same time "sends back" those in the distance.

The sparse foliage will not be difficult to imitate by those who have practised the earlier lessons. The shading of the trunks is produced almost entirely by the horizontal shading of a *rounded* chisel-point. This has the effect of conveying to the eye the smooth surface of the Beech's bark. The pale tint is laid on first with a B. pencil; the middle tint and final detail being done with a B.B. pencil. The moss and lichens that adhere to the interstices of the bark, both at the base of the trunk and where the main branches spring from it, give rich markings, which express well the muscular indentations of its surface. These are very important to the correct delineation of the tree.

This is a very beautiful drawing, we think perhaps one of the best that has come to us from Mr. Needham's pencil. We hope to see many good copies of this subject, not only in pencil but in colors by and by.

These Beeches have not suffered from the destructive process of "pollarding," and stand proudly in their natural beauty, like a line of hale hardy veterans guarding the outskirts of the forest. Several lines of equally symmetrical Beeches are to be found on the outskirts of Burnham Wood. Why so many trees within its recesses were tortured and mangled, or at what period this was done, is unknown.

However, these mutilated trees are not devoid of beauty, and a certain weird grandeur is evident in the drawing of an old Beech on page 46. Before copying it let it be well studied. The trunk is almost a *fasciculus* of trees—like a whole family of Beeches bound together. This peculiarity of growth gives vertical lines to contrast with the horizontal shading of the bark, and cuts up the huge trunk into perpendicular masses, adding much to its picturesque effect and also helping the student to copy it. A very careful sketch should be made, tracing the course of the boughs, and placing the twigs and branches so as to carry the foliage as in nature. The distance must be kept delicate. The practice in the first lesson of foliage should make that part simple enough, and the trunk and stems are but repetitions of what we have already advised for the example on page 45.

The drawing of the ancient Beech trunk, on page 47, exhibits a tree of still more

ROW OF BEECHES, BURNHAM. Drawn by J. NEEDHAM.

IN BURNHAM BEECHES.—Drawn by J. NEEDHAM.

IN BURNHAM BEECHES.—Drawn by J. Needham.

venerable aspect. We anticipate no difficulty in copying it after the practice in the earlier studies. The old trunk is varied with growths of deeply tinted lichens, which give its hoary surface the color it requires for contrast with the fresh vigorous boughs that spring from it. The old stump seems to take a new lease of life and bud forth anew. The delicate soft touch of the young spring foliage must be well imitated, and the whole drawing kept as soft and light as possible to indicate brightness and refinement of effect. The distance especially must be kept pale, to contribute the airy character to the picture.

PAINTING THE BEECH.—THE COLORED ILLUSTRATIONS.

W E have already adverted to the painting of the sprays of the Beech, and have to request that the examples of brush-work given on page 13 may be fully mastered before the work of the present larger studies be attempted. This done, the picture of the OLD BEECH-TRUNKS IN BURNHAM WOOD (Plate IX.) will occupy our attention. We would enjoin our pupils to keep in mind the necessity of making a very careful outline sketch of our subject, which is worthy of close study, before beginning to color it. The horizontal markings of the almost polished bark are very true to nature, and must be imitated with delicate precision. It will be well to lay in these grey markings (Light Red and Black) before any other coloring (save the first warm wash to the whole paper) is applied. The faint blue sky, the middle distance, and the deep shadow of the wooded valley can receive its Neutral Tint at the same time. A faint wash of Light Red and a little Olive Green can be given to the entire surface of the trunks, varying the tint, however, where the highest lights appear. A little Vandyke Brown will be required to give the warmer hue to the ground from which the trees spring, and to some of the warmer parts of the trunks themselves. Here and there the mossy lichen-covered bark will require some Olive Green embrowned with a little Sepia. When this is quite dry, some Yellow Ochre may be painted in, to form the ground tint of sunlight shining through the deeper touches of foliage, and in some parts of the trunk which catch or reflect the warm sunlight. Yellow Ochre, Cobalt, and Sepia will supply the colors for the warm parts of the foliage in the hollow, and also for the shadows in the lower part of it.

In order to test if the upper parts of the largest trunk have arrived at sufficient depth of color, it may be well now to paint in the foliage (Olive Green and Indigo), gradually deepening the tints by varying the greens in the manner already described. It is probable that the juxtaposition of the foliage will show that the trunk and large branches require some strengthening in their various colors. Last of all, the detail of the little crevices (Vandyke Brown or in some cases Sepia) will be applied, with a very finely pointed brush. Some parts of the moss-grown bark may still require a little more dull Olive Green.

The more finished picture of the BEECH IN EARLY AUTUMN (Plate VIII. page 43) will next claim our pupil's attention. When the early frosts of autumn first make their appearance, the foliage of one of those trees whose situation is more exposed than others, is apt to be withered with the blast of approaching winter, and we frequently see the side of the tree which is next the prevailing wind thus assume the tints of autumn rather prematurely.

PLATE IX.—OLD BEECH TRUNKS IN BURNHAM WOOD.— By J. NEEDHAM.

We are glad that our artist has thus afforded our pupils a bit of practice in the gorgeous hues of autumn. Again, let us insist upon the necessity of a careful sketch being made with every detail as perfect as possible. The sky is painted with some Cobalt, Lamp Black, and Light Red, and the whole must get a faint wash of Yellow Ochre. The distance and warm tints underlying the foreground had better all be laid in before the painting of the main tree is attempted; all can be done with Yellow Ochre, Cobalt, and Black, in varying quantities. The middle distance will require Light Red also, and so will part of the foreground.

The neutral tints used for the sky and distance can also be employed to underlie the shaded parts of the foliage and trunk. The lesson in foliage (pages 13 and 14) will come useful to convey the touch, though the colors may vary for the warm side of the tree from those specified for the first practice. A wash of Yellow Ochre underlies the warm-tinted foliage, the trunk, and the ground. This may have to be repeated several times in parts of the foliage, each time retiring a little from the edges of the sprays so as to leave the effect of the light catching their extreme edges. A little Raw Sienna will be added to the Yellow Ochre to express the reddish-yellow boughs, and this may have to be used several times for the deeper parts.

The parts of the foliage which still retain the tint of their summer verdure will require varying greens, all of which can be rendered by combinations of Brown Pink and Indigo tinged with a little Gamboge for the parts in high light and Raw Sienna sparingly added, with a little Vandyke Brown for the detail of the parts in shadow; a little pale Olive Green will be applied to tone the greys on part of the trunk. The warm color of the foreground will require Brown Pink, and some Brown Madder and Indian Yellow to enrich it, with a little French Ultramarine to impart the grass green. Some bold touches of Vandyke Brown may even still be required for the strong shadows on the trunk, branches, and where the roots penetrate the ground. These must be carefully imitated; if overdone in depth the drawing will look spotty. The shepherd forms a useful object to give transparence, by contrast, at once to the shadow of the tree and distance to the landscape.

If the young painter have not been able to "save out" the little masses of light that are intended to represent the sheep, he may now, by the use of a little water, clean blotting-paper, and wash-leather, remedy the defect. In the same manner where the tips of the spray tell out against the shadowed trunk, and may not have been "saved," he may now pick them out; and if he is not able to do it sharply enough, both these finishing touches (and any little bits of light missing from his other sprays) may be now supplied by careful minute touches of Chinese White, toned down with a little Light Red and Naples Yellow. But these last efforts to conceal defects must be very sparingly adopted, and it would be better if carefulness in imitation of the original would allow them to be dispensed with entirely.

Having practised the drawing of the Oak, Ash, and Beech, our pupils can now be trusted to attempt drawing from nature. Two facsimiles of studies from nature, to show the amount of work that should be allowed in bold rapid sketching, will be found on pages 51, 52. These subjects have already been fully described when treating of the sketching of the Oak.

OAK—FACSIMILE OF A SKETCH FROM NATURE.—Drawn by J. NEEDHAM.

OLD OAK-TRUNK—FACSIMILE OF A SKETCH FROM NATURE.—Drawn by J. NEEDHAM.

VERE FOSTER'S WATER-COLOR BOOKS.

PAINTING FOR BEGINNERS.—First Stage.

Teaching the use of One Color. Ten Facsimiles of Original Studies in Sepia, by J. CALLOW, and numerous Illustrations in Pencil. With full instructions in easy language. In Three Parts 4to, 6d. each; or one volume, cloth elegant, 2s. 6d.

PAINTING FOR BEGINNERS.—Second Stage.

Teaching the use of Seven Colors. Twenty Facsimiles of Original Drawings by J. CALLOW, and many Illustrations in Pencil. With full instructions in easy language. In Six Parts 4to, 6d. each; or one volume, cloth elegant, 4s.

SIMPLE LESSONS IN FLOWER PAINTING.

Eight Facsimiles of Original Water-Color Drawings, and numerous Outline Drawings of Flowers, after various artists. With full instructions for Drawing and Painting. In Four Parts 4to, 6d. each; or one volume, cloth elegant, 3s.

"Everything necessary for acquiring the art of flower painting is here; the *facsimiles* of water-color drawings are very beautiful."—*Graphic*.

"Such excellent books, so carefully written and studied, cannot fail to have great advantage in the creation and fostering of a taste for art."—*Scotsman*.

SIMPLE LESSONS IN MARINE PAINTING.

Twelve Facsimiles of Original Water-Color Sketches. By EDWARD DUNCAN. With numerous Illustrations in Pencil, and Practical Lessons by an experienced Master. In Four Parts 4to, 6d. each; or one volume, cloth elegant, 3s.

"The book on Marine Painting must prove of great value to students. Nothing could be prettier or more charming than the sketches here presented."—*Graphic*.

"The possession of a box of water-colors, a sketch block, and this volume of Simple Lessons will add a new and a very real pleasure indeed to a visit to the sea-side."—*Knowledge*.

SIMPLE LESSONS IN LANDSCAPE PAINTING.

Eight Facsimiles of Original Water-Color Drawings, and Thirty Vignettes, after various artists. With full instructions by an experienced Master. In Four Parts 4to, 6d. each; or one volume, cloth elegant, 3s.

"As a work of art in the book line we have seldom seen its equal; and it could not fail to be a delightful present, affording a great amount of pleasurable amusement and instruction, to young people."—*St. James's Gazette*.

EASY STUDIES IN WATER-COLOR PAINTING.

By R. P. LEITCH, and J. CALLOW. A Series of Nine Pictures executed in Neutral Tints. With full instructions for drawing each subject, and for sketching from Nature. In Three Parts 4to, 1s. 6d. each; or one volume, cloth elegant, 6s.

SKETCHES IN WATER-COLORS.

By T. M. RICHARDSON, R. P. LEITCH, J. A. HOUSTON, T. L. ROWBOTHAM, F. DUNCAN, and J. NEEDHAM. A Series of Nine Pictures executed in Colors. With full instructions for drawing each subject, by an experienced Teacher. In Three Parts 4to, 1s. 6d. each; or one volume, cloth elegant, 6s.

"The names of the artists are quite sufficient to stamp these books with the highest qualities. The pictures are judicious in selection and artistic in execution, while the instructions are so full and clear as to almost supersede the need of a teacher."—*Liverpool Courier*.

STUDIES OF TREES.

In Pencil and in Water-Colors, by J. NEEDHAM. A Series of Eighteen Examples in Colors, and Thirty-three Drawings in Pencil. With descriptions of the Trees, and full instructions for Drawing and Painting. In Eight Parts 4to, 1s. each; or First Series, cloth elegant, 5s.; Second Series, cloth elegant, 5s.

LONDON: BLACKIE & SON; GLASGOW, EDINBURGH, AND DUBLIN.

Adopted by the Science and Art Department, South Kensington.

VERE FOSTER'S DRAWING COPY-BOOKS.

GRADED AND PROGRESSIVE,

WITH INSTRUCTIONS AND PAPER TO DRAW ON.

IN TWELVE PARTS AT ONE SHILLING EACH.

Part I.—ELEMENTARY LESSONS.	*Part V.*—TREES IN LEAD PENCIL.	*Part IX.*—ANIMALS, by H. WEIR (*continued*).
Part II.—OBJECTS WITH CURVED LINES.	*Part VI.*—LANDSCAPE IN LEAD PENCIL.	*Part X.*—HUMAN FIGURE.
Part III.—PLANTS AND FLOWERS	*Part VII.*—MARINE, by CALLOW, &c.	*Part XI.*—PRACTICAL GEOMETRY.
Part IV.—ORNAMENT, by F. E. HULME.	*Part VIII.*—ANIMALS, by H. WEIR.	*Part XII.*—MECHANICAL DRAWING.

PUBLISHED ALSO IN FIFTY NUMBERS AT THREEPENCE EACH.

ELEMENTARY LESSONS.

A 1 Initiatory Lessons.
A 2 Letters and Numerals.
B 1 Objects (Straight Lines).
B 2 Domestic Objects (Simple).

OBJECTS WITH CURVED LINES.

C 1 Domestic Objects (Flat Treatment).
C 2 Domestic Objects (Perspective)
D 1 Leaves (Flat Treatment).
D 2 Leaves (Natural Treatment).

PLANTS AND FLOWERS.

E 1 Plants (Simple Forms).
E 2 Plants (Advanced).
G 1 Flowers (Simple Forms).
G 2 Flowers (Advanced).

ORNAMENT, by F. E. HULME.

I 1 Elementary Forms.
I 2 Simple Forms (Fretwork, &c.).
I 3 Advanced Forms (Carving, &c.).
I 4 Ornament (Classic, &c.).

TREES IN LEAD PENCIL.

J 1 Oak, Fir, &c
J 2 Beech, Elm, &c.
J 3 Oak, Chestnut, Birch.
J 4 Birch, Larch, Poplar, &c.

LANDSCAPE IN LEAD PENCIL.

K 1 Rustic Landscape in Outline.
K 2 Shaded Objects, &c.
K 3 Shaded Landscape.
K 4 Advanced Landscape.

MARINE, by CALLOW, &c.

M 1 Boats, Foregrounds, &c.
M 2 Fishing Craft, Coasters, &c.
M 3 Yachts and other Vessels.
M 4 Drawing of Waves.

HUMAN FIGURE.

Q 1 Features.
Q 2 Heads, Hands, &c.
Q 3 Rustic Figures, by Duncan.
Q 4 Figure from the Antique.
Z   Blank Exercise Book.

ANIMALS, by H. WEIR.

O 1 Birds and Quadrupeds.
O 2 Poultry, various breeds.
O 3 British Small Birds.
O 4 British Wild Animals.
O 5 Horses (Arab, Hunter, &c.).
O 6 Horses (Racer, Trotter, &c.).
O 7 Dogs (Seventeen Species).
O 8 Cattle, Sheep, Pigs, &c.
O 9 Lambs, Ass, Foal, &c.
O 10 Foreign Animals, &c.

PRACTICAL GEOMETRY.

R 1 Definitions and Simple Problems.
R 2 Practical Geometry.
R 3 Applied Geometry.

PRACTICAL MECHANICAL DRAWING.

T 1 Initiatory.
T 2 Details of Tools, &c.
T 3 Models for Working Drawings, &c.
T 4 Details of Machines and Engines.

VERE FOSTER'S DRAWING CARDS.

BEAUTIFULLY PRINTED ON FINE CARDS AND DONE UP IN NEAT PACKETS.

First Grade, Set I.—FAMILIAR OBJECTS, 24 cards, 1*s.*

First Grade, Set II.—LEAF FORM, 24 cards, price 1*s.*

First Grade, Set III.—ELEMENTARY ORNAMENT, 24 cards, price 1*s.*

Second Grade.—ORNAMENT, by F. E. HULME, 18 large cards, price 2*s.*

Advanced Series.—ANIMALS, by HARRISON WEIR, 24 cards, price 1*s. 6d.*

OF VERE FOSTER'S DRAWING-BOOKS

The STANDARD says—There is no book of instruction in drawing, no matter what its price, so well calculated to aid self-help as Vere Foster's books. Even in schools that possess the advantage of apt and experienced teachers of drawing, their advantages will speedily become manifest. Mr. Vere Foster has done a public service by the production of this series.

The GRAPHIC says—If any parent who reads these lines has a boy or girl who wishes to learn how to be an artist, let us boldly recommend Vere Foster's Drawing-Book. It is not only the cheapest, but by far the best that we have seen.

The ART JOURNAL says—It would be difficult to overrate the value of this work—a work that is not to be estimated by its cost: one is great, the other very small. Any learner may find in it a huge volume of thought, his studies rightly directed by a competent practical teacher, who will teach him nothing by which he can be led astray, or that he will have to unlearn when he consults the great Book of Nature.

LONDON: BLACKIE & SON; GLASGOW, EDINBURGH, AND DUBLIN.

POYNTER'S SOUTH KENSINGTON DRAWING-BOOK.

THIS New Series of Drawing Copies has been issued under the direct superintendence of E. J. POYNTER, R.A. The examples have been selected for the most part from objects in the SOUTH KENSINGTON MUSEUM, and the Drawings have been made under Mr. Poynter's careful personal supervision by Pupils of the NATIONAL ART TRAINING SCHOOL.

Each Book has Fine Cartridge Paper to draw on.

Two Books. ELEMENTARY FREEHAND DRAWING. Sixpence Each.

I.—SIMPLE GEOMETRICAL FORMS. | II.—CONVENTIONALIZED FLORAL FORMS.

Six Books. FREEHAND DRAWING, ORNAMENT, FIRST GRADE. Sixpence Each.

I.—SIMPLE OBJECTS AND ORNAMENT—*Flat.*
II.—VARIOUS OBJECTS—*Flat.*
III.—OBJECTS AND ARCHITECTURAL ORNAMENT—*Flat and Perspective.*

IV.—ARCHITECTURAL ORNAMENT—*Flat.*
V. — OBJECTS OF GLASS AND EARTHENWARE — *Perspective.*
VI.—COMMON OBJECTS—*Perspective.*

Six Books. FREEHAND DRAWING, PLANTS, FIRST GRADE. Sixpence Each.

I.—LEAVES AND FLOWERS—*Simplest.* | III.—FLOWERS, FRUITS, &c. | V.—FLOWERS.
II.—LEAVES, FLOWERS, FRUITS. | IV.—FLOWERS AND FOLIAGE. | VI.—FLOWERS.

Four Books. FREEHAND DRAWING, SECOND GRADE. One Shilling Each.

I.—FORMS OF ANTHEMION ORNAMENT, &c.—*Flat.*
II.—GREEK, ROMAN, AND VENETIAN—*Flat and Perspective.*

III.—ITALIAN RENAISSANCE—*Flat.*
IV.—ROMAN, ITALIAN, JAPANESE, &c.—*Flat and Perspective.*

THE SAME SUBJECTS ON CARDS.

Elementary Freehand (Cards), ...	...	...	...	..	Four Packets, Price 9d. each.			
First Grade, Freehand Ornament (Cards), ...	...	...	Six	„	„	1/	„	
First Grade, Freehand Plants (Cards),	...	...	...	Six	„	„	1/	„
Second Grade, Freehand (Cards),	...	...	...	Four	„	„	1/6	„

Four Books. ELEMENTARY HUMAN FIGURE. Sixpence Each.

I.—MICHELANGELO'S "DAVID"—Features. | III.—HANDS, FROM SCULPTURE.
II.—MASKS, FROM ANTIQUE SCULPTURE. | IV.—FEET, FROM SCULPTURE.

Three Books. ADVANCED HUMAN FIGURE. Imp. 4to, Two Shillings Each.

Book I.—HEAD OF THE VENUS OF MELOS.
Book II.—HEAD OF THE YOUTHFUL BACCHUS.
Book III.—HEAD OF DAVID BY MICHELANGELO.

Four Books. FIGURES FROM THE CARTOONS OF RAPHAEL. Imp. 4to, 2s. Each.

Twelve Studies of Draped Figures. Drawn direct from the Originals in the South Kensington Museum. With Descriptive Text, and Paper for Copying.

Four Books, 1s. Each. ELEMENTARY PERSPECTIVE DRAWING. One Vol., cloth, 5s.

By S. J. CARTLIDGE, F.R.Hist.S., Lecturer in the National Art Training School, South Kensington.

Book I. ⎰
Book II. ⎱ For Second Grade Examination of the Department.

Book III.—ACCIDENTAL VANISHING POINTS.
Book IV.—HIGHER PERSPECTIVE.

The PALL MALL GAZETTE says:

" The choice of subjects is admirable; there is not an ugly drawing in the book. Parents and teachers who have been looking in vain for drawing-books that should really train the eye in the study of beautiful forms, as well as the hand in the representation of what the eye sees, will be very grateful to the Science and Art Department for these cheap and most satisfactory productions."

LONDON: BLACKIE & SON; GLASGOW, EDINBURGH, AND DUBLIN.

BLACKIE & SON'S BOOKS FOR THE YOUNG.

Price 7s. 6d.

The Universe: Or the Infinitely Great and the Infinitely Little. A Sketch of Contrasts in Creation and Marvels revealed and explained by Nature and Science. By F. A. POUCHET, M.D. With 273 Engravings on wood. 8th Edition, medium 8vo, cloth elegant, gilt edges.

Price 6s.

True to the Old Flag: A Tale of the American War of Independence. By G. A. HENTY. With 12 full-page Illustrations by GORDON BROWNE. Cloth elegant, olivine edges.

In Freedom's Cause: A Story of Wallace and Bruce. By G. A. HENTY. With 12 full-page Illustrations by GORDON BROWNE. Cloth elegant, olivine edges.

With Clive in India: Or the Beginnings of an Empire. By G. A. HENTY. With 12 full-page Illustrations by GORDON BROWNE. Cloth elegant, olivine edges.

Bunyip Land: The Story of a Wild Journey in New Guinea. By G. MANVILLE FENN. With 12 full-page Illustrations by GORDON BROWNE. Cloth elegant, olivine edges.

The Golden Magnet: A Tale of the Land of the Incas. By GEO. MANVILLE FENN. With 12 full-page Pictures by GORDON BROWNE. Cloth elegant, olivine edges.

The Life and Surprising Adventures of Robinson Crusoe. By DANIEL DEFOE. Beautifully Printed, and Illustrated by above 100 Pictures designed by GORDON BROWNE. Cloth elegant, olivine edges. [Reprinted from the Author's Edition.]

In the King's Name: Or the Cruise of the *Kestrel*. By GEO. MANVILLE FENN. With 12 full-page Pictures by GORDON BROWNE. Cloth elegant, olivine edges.

Under Drake's Flag. A Tale of the Spanish Main. By G. A. HENTY. With 12 full-page Pictures by GORDON BROWNE. Cloth elegant, olivine edges.

Price 5s.

St. George for England: A Tale of Cressy and Poitiers. By G. A. HENTY. With 8 full-page Illustrations. Cl. elegant.

Menhardoc: A Story of Cornish Nets and Mines. By G. MANVILLE FENN. With 8 full-page Illustrations. Cl. elegant.

The Pirate Island: A Story of the South Pacific. By HARRY COLLINGWOOD. With 8 full-page Pictures. Cloth elegant.

The Wigwam and the Warpath; Stories of the Red Indians. By ASCOTT R. HOPE. With 8 full-page Pictures. Cloth elegant.

By Sheer Pluck; A Tale of the Ashanti War. By G. A. HENTY. With 8 full-page Illustrations. Cloth elegant.

Stories of Old Renown. Tales of Knights and Heroes. By ASCOTT R. HOPE. With 100 Illustrations by GORDON BROWNE. Cloth elegant, olivine edges.

Facing Death: Or the Hero of the Vaughan Pit. By G. A. HENTY. With 8 full-page Illustrations. Cloth elegant.

Nat the Naturalist: Or a Boy's Adventures in the Eastern Seas. By GEO. MANVILLE FENN. With 8 full-page Pictures. Cloth elegant.

Price 3s. 6d.

Cheep and Chatter; Or Lessons from Field and Tree. By ALICE BANKS. With 54 Character Illustrations by GORDON BROWNE. Cloth elegant. With gilt edges, 4s.

The Wreck of the Nancy Bell: Or Cast away on Kerguelen Land. By JOHN C. HUTCHESON. Illustrated by 6 full-page Pictures. Cloth extra.

Picked up at Sea: Or the Gold Miners of Minturne Creek. By JOHN C. HUTCHESON. With 6 full-page Pictures in Tints. Cloth extra.

Dr. Jolliffe's Boys: A Tale of Weston School. By LEWIS HOUGH. With 6 full-page Pictures. Cloth extra.

Traitor or Patriot? A Tale of the Rye-House Plot. By MARY C. ROWSELL. Illustrated by 6 full-page Pictures. Cloth elegant.

Brother and Sister: Or the Trials of the Moore Family. By ELIZABETH J. LYSAGHT. With 6 full-page Illustrations. Cloth extra.

Dora: Or a Girl without a Home. By Mrs. R. H. READ. With 6 full-page Illustrations. Cloth extra.

Garnered Sheaves. A Tale for Boys. By Mrs. EMMA R. PITMAN. With 4 full-page Illustrations. Cloth extra.

Florence Godfrey's Faith. A Story of Australian Life. By Mrs. PITMAN. With 4 full-page Illustrations. Cloth extra.

Life's Daily Ministry. A Story of Everyday Service for Others. By Mrs. EMMA R. PITMAN. With 4 full-page Illustrations. Cloth extra.

My Governess Life: Or Earning my Living. By Mrs. EMMA R. PITMAN. With 4 full-page Illustrations. Cloth extra.

Price 2s. 6d.

Each book is beautifully illustrated, and bound in cloth extra.

Brothers in Arms: A Story of the Crusades. By F. BAYFORD HARRISON.

Jack o' Lanthorn. A Tale of Adventure. By HENRY FRITH.

Winnie's Secret: A Story of Faith and Patience. By KATE WOOD.

A Waif of the Sea: Or the Lost Found. By KATE WOOD.

Hetty Gray, or Nobody's Bairn. By ROSA MULHOLLAND.

Miss Fenwick's Failures: Or "Peggy Pepper-pot." By ESMÉ STUART.

The Ball of Fortune; Or Ned Somerset's Inheritance. By CHARLES PEARCE.

The Family Failing. By DARLEY DALE.

Stories of the Sea in Former Days; Narratives of Wreck and Rescue.

Adventures in Field, Flood, and Forest; Stories of Danger and Daring.

LONDON: BLACKIE & SON, 49 & 50 OLD BAILEY, E.C.;
GLASGOW, EDINBURGH, AND DUBLIN.

Lightning Source UK Ltd.
Milton Keynes UK
UKHW010720120822
407216UK00005B/427